Grace Encounters

A Bible Study

Grace Encounters

A Bible Study

Marjie Schaefer

"Of the fullness of
His grace, we have all
received — grace upon
grace, grace upon grace."
(John 1:16)

with grace & peace,
Marjie
Schaefer

Paradise
Creek
Books

Paradise Creek Books
Elgin, Iowa and Seattle, Washington

Paradise Creek Books
www.paradisecreekbooks.com

Unless otherwise noted, Scripture quotations are from *The New Spirit Filled Life Bible*. Copyright ©2002, Thomas Nelson, Inc., Publisher; and *The Holy Bible*, New King James Version. Copyright ©1982, Thomas Nelson, Inc.

Scripture quotations noted Amplified are from *The Amplified Bible, Expanded Edition.* Copyright ©1987, Zondervan Corporation and the Lockman Foundation.

Scripture quotations noted Heb-Greek are from *The Hebrew-Greek Key Word Study Bible,* King James Version. Copyright ©1984, 1991, AMG International, Inc.

Scripture quotations noted Message are from *The Message: The New Testament in Contemporary English.* Copyright ©1993, Eugene H. Peterson.

Printed in the United States of America

First Publication: August 2011

ISBN # 978-0-9836652-3-6

Book Producer and Editor: Candace Sinclair
Cover Designer: Stephanie Fox
Interior Design: Stephanie Fox

Ordering Information

Special discounts are available on quantity purchases. For details, contact Paradise Creek Books at the web address above.

Table of Contents

Dedication

I am profoundly grateful for the life I enjoy and celebrate with my husband, Steve, and children, Hayley, Jordan, Matthew, and Luke.

This Bible study is lovingly dedicated to these five people who make up the group we call family. Our life together is sometimes crazy and a bit unpredictable, but always set in the context of Grace.

Thanks to all of you for teaching me a little bit more about what grace means.

Acknowledgments

Through the writing of this Bible study, I have learned things about Jesus, His love for me, His compassion and mercy toward me, and His divine enablement of me that have indeed transformed my life. Because of this, I love Him more and more and I am overwhelmed and motivated by *His* love and grace in my life. It is my earnest desire to express this passion for my Lord as I seek to teach this study to the women He brings across my path.

This study highlights five women in the Bible who encountered Grace—Jesus Christ. I want to acknowledge five women who I know have also encountered Grace and have been transformed by His touch.

My sister, **Leigh Laird**, is a woman who earnestly and consistently longs for as much of Jesus and His grace and power in her life as she can get. She is like that woman pressing through the throngs of people to get to Jesus to "touch the hem of His garment." She will not stop until she can receive more of Him and all that He offers. She longs to share Him with others, too—especially those closest to her: her husband and children. Leigh is a beautiful example of a woman who hungers and thirsts after Jesus.

Christine Carlin, a friend of many years now, is definitely a woman who has encountered Grace Personified—Jesus Christ. Her life of grace and graciousness is like a beautiful garden, tended to by the Master

Gardener Himself. She is a fruitful branch attached to the True Vine, consistently revealing love for Christ and others and great faith, and thus an ever-increasing knowledge and revelation of Jesus displayed by multiplied grace and peace.

Debbie Frolander and **Lisa Steele** have both inspired me and challenged me with their bedrock faith in the grace of Jesus Christ. Both of these dear friends have journeyed through a "desert" in recent years, yet they have never given up or taken their eyes off of Jesus—the Author and Finisher of their faith. These two precious friends are "trophies" of His grace and have only begun to see the Lord's blessing and goodness poured out in their lives.

My friend, **Donna Sandberg**, is another woman of grace, and one who reminds me of Mary of Bethany—constantly sitting at the feet of Jesus as a learner and a worshiper. As a result of being in the Presence of Jesus, her speech, demeanor, and interactions with others consistently reveal her Lord and Savior. She speaks the Word of God in almost every conversation, and that's because the Word permeates her life. Donna is a beautiful example to me and everyone who knows her, of what grace looks like "fleshed out."

A Personal Note from Marjie

I am delighted that you have chosen to be part of the *Grace Encounters* Bible study. It is my earnest prayer that you will complete the Bible study and discover yourself more in love with your Lord and Savior, Jesus Christ, than you ever have been before.

My personal request of you is to prayerfully allow yourself enough time to sit at your Savior's feet each day and to learn from Him. Mary of Bethany knew that this was the key to life. She opted out of her societal hospitality demands and cultural mores of her day to just sit and soak up Jesus. Jesus commended her for this and declared that no one would ever be able to take that away from her—she had chosen the *best* thing.

This is my prayer for all of us as we embark on this journey of "grace." There is so much for all of us to learn and to soak up. Many Scriptures are provided for you each day. Please look up each one and ask the Holy Spirit to "quicken the Word" to you as you read, study, and meditate.

There are also extra comments and various exercises provided for you throughout the study. The old cliché is true: *you will get as much out of it as you put into it.* My recommendation is to carve out at least an hour for yourself each day to complete the study.

Each week has five days' worth of Bible study. Throughout each week, there are sections entitled "Questions for Reflection." This is meant to be a time for you to answer those questions in light of what you've studied and in a spirit of prayer, allowing the Lord to search your heart and to teach you.

You will also discover promptings for deliberate times of prayer and worship sprinkled throughout the study. Take time to worship your Lord, and might I add, to praise Him *out loud*. Make your Scriptural declarations audible, for "faith comes by hearing and hearing by the Word of God." (Romans 10:17)

When your ears hear your mouth declare the Word, your life will be transformed as your faith grows, and as your belief in *who you are in Christ* gets confirmed by the very Word of God.

Welcome to the study! Make yourself a cup of tea or coffee, and let's get started.

May you know and experience the fullness of His grace more and more each day.

~Marjie

What is *Grace Encounters* All About?

You are embarking on a journey where you will peer into the lives of five different women in the Bible who met Jesus face-to-face. These women had the encounter of their lives, and they were forever transformed because of it.

The *process* of your journey is as important as the journey itself. All of the studying, including looking up each verse, reading, thinking, writing, praying, meditating on each person and each touch from Jesus is part and parcel of the all-encompassing process, which will ultimately take you to a destination ordained by God, just for you!

The truth is, you could spend weeks studying each woman. The woman at the well, for example, has many different aspects to her conversation with Jesus and the end result of that conversation. You could spend months studying her encounter.

Because it's Jesus we're talking about, the encounters are deep and life-changing. We cannot plumb the depths of all there is to learn and glean from the Word—the Living Word, Jesus. My hope is that these studies involving these women who meet Jesus will serve as a springboard for you to go deeper into your personal study of the Word.

Before you jump into this particular study on grace, it is important to take a Biblical look at the word grace and further investigate what grace really means for your daily life.

I don't know if you're like me, but I grew up in church and sang about grace all of my life. But somewhere along the way, I compartmentalized grace and relegated it to that category of what happened to me when I first met Jesus and encountered Him for myself.

Ephesians 2:8 in the Amplified Bible says, "For it is by free grace (God's unmerited favor) that you are saved (delivered from judgment and made partakers of Christ's salvation) through (your) faith. And this (salvation) is not of yourselves (of your own doing, it came not through your own striving), but it is the gift of God."

This is the starting point of grace in the life of a believer. Grace is God's unmerited favor. It is unearned and free—a gift that we receive simply by faith.

I love that phrase "it came not through your own striving." There is nothing I can do to get it, buy it, work for it, earn it, or strive for it. No effort, labor, willpower, or exertion will ever bring grace into my life. It is unmerited and has nothing to do with me—that's why it's amazing!

For me, being a good "church girl," this was easy to believe and accept in regard to my own saving faith through Jesus. I know I can't earn my own salvation, and I'm very happy about that! I'm thankful that it's not up to me. But what I have come to see and understand about all of this is that just as my salvation continues throughout my life, grace continues as well. Grace is so much more than God's forgiveness of me through the atoning death of Jesus on the cross.

Grace is so much more than just God's disposition toward me. Grace is God, meeting me at my point of need through the Person of Jesus

Christ—including all of His power and provision. (This definition is attributed to Jack Hayford.)

In other words, I am saved by grace, but I live by grace every day. If I received the gift of salvation by grace and I believe that it was all His work, what makes me think that I have to work for or earn His other blessings?

I receive His grace based on His finished work on the cross and not through my own striving. I don't ever have to earn His approval or His favor, because I already have it. The Bible is replete with proof texts regarding this, and you will discover some of them on your journey. Please know this as you begin: You have the Lord's favor and approval because of Jesus' finished work on the cross.

The Greek word for grace is ***charis*** (pronounced *kharece*). It means divine favor and blessing; that which affords joy, pleasure, delight, sweetness, charm, and loveliness; grace of speech; goodwill; loving-kindness; the divine influence upon the heart and its reflection in the life manifested in gratitude.

Romans 8:31 says, "What then shall we say…if God is for us, who can be against us?"

God is for us right now because of His grace. God sent His Son to die for us, and Jesus gave us a blood-bought right to an abundant life, full of meaning and purpose. We have abundant life, not because we deserve it, but because of grace—because God is for us.

The very name of Jesus—Immanuel—means that He is with us.

Therefore, not only is God for me, but He is *with* me. This doesn't mean I won't have struggles, issues, or face unexpected events in my life, but His grace—His unmerited favor and blessing—His divine influence at work in my life, is carrying me through it all.

Galatians 2:20–21 in the Amplified Bible has come to mean so much to me through my own journey of discovery of grace:

"I have been crucified with Christ (in Him I have shared His crucifixion); it is no longer I who live, but Christ (the Messiah) lives in me; and the life I now live in the body I live by faith in (by adherence to and reliance on and complete trust in) the Son of God, Who loved me and gave Himself up for me.

(Therefore, I do not treat God's gracious gift as something of minor importance and defeat its very purpose); I do not set aside (and invalidate and frustrate and nullify) the grace (unmerited favor) of God. For if justification (righteousness, acquittal from guilt) comes through (observing the ritual of) the Law, then Christ the Messiah died groundlessly and to no purpose and in vain (His death was then wholly superfluous)."

In other words, if I want God's promises to be sure in my life, I can't depend on myself, my obedience, my goodness, my service, or even my faith—it's all grace. It's all God's unmerited favor in my life and nothing that I do at all. My trust needs to be placed in His goodness and His Word and not in my behavior.

Paul declared in the Galatians passage that "I have been crucified with Christ." This is really where our journey of grace starts—at the cross.

Because the Lord Jesus was crucified over 2,000 years ago, as a believer and now follower of Christ, I was crucified with Him. This is an historic fact. His experience has become my spiritual history.

My Christian life begins with the discovery of what God has provided for me in Christ alone. I rest in the finished work of Christ on the cross. A single sovereign act of God that brought together all the guilt and suffering of humanity in one climactic moment of time meets every need you and I will ever encounter. Every need is met in the Person of Jesus. God has not provided many different solutions for the multitudes of problems we will encounter. He offers us one all-sufficient solution: Jesus Christ and His complete work upon the cross.

Jesus Christ took my place of no protection at the cross. He gave up divine protection so that I can have it every day of my life. Because He became sin, He took my curse at the cross so that today I can take His gift of righteousness.

It's as if God Himself is saying to me, "When My Son was crucified, you were in Him, so now His experience has become your spiritual history. All shame, guilt, rejection, fear, and insecurity has been dealt with. My wrath has been poured out and completely satisfied. In My records, your sins are wiped clean. And My records are the only ones that count."

Today it's important for all of us to know that God is not mad at us. The body of Jesus Christ absorbed His wrath on our behalf. Paul made that clear when he told us in Galatians that he had been crucified with Christ. Jesus took all of what was rightfully deserved by us so that now our expectation is one of grace. I don't really like to use the word "should," but in this case, it's probably all right—we should all live in the expectation of the goodness of God every day. Today, if you are a believer and a follower of Jesus Christ, your expectation should be one of grace.

Welcome to *Grace Encounters*. May you encounter the One Who made it all possible for you.

Lesson 1: Grace Quenches

Week One - Day 1: Encounter at the Well

John 4:4–42

Before you begin…

Prayerfully ask the Lord to speak to you specifically and definitely through His Word. Ask the Lord to "quicken you according to His Word" (Ps. 119:250)

You are about to enter the nation of Samaria, a land despised by the Jews. In this lesson, you will learn how Jesus purposely planned His trip to go through this land in light of His divine encounter with the woman at the well.

This woman is not a person who was widely accepted in the town, given her immoral lifestyle. She plans her trips to the well on purpose, too, in order to avoid the crowds of those who disregard her. But Jesus takes the time to engage her on a personal level, telling her about the "living water" not found in any well and revealing to her the saving grace available to her, despite her lifestyle choices.

I encourage you to take the time to look up each verse and reference provided for you here in order to glean as much as you can from this encounter. As you do this, you will be encouraged to see that the one who avoided the crowds becomes the one who brings the crowds to Jesus.

The Holy Spirit, true worship, *Zoe* life, and a healthy branch attached to the "Vine" are the predominant themes in this week's study. While these may be familiar to you, they become fresh and new again set in the context of this personal encounter.

* * *

Read the story of the woman at the well in John 4:4–42. Reading this encounter in its entirety will enable you to have the context as we "exegete" *(discover the meaning of the text objectively and moving out from there)* the text and story to glean as much as you can from it.

What specific aspects of this encounter jump out at you from your reading? List them here:

As Jesus asks the woman for a drink (v.7), her immediate response is, "How is it that you, a Jew, asks a Samaritan for a drink?" (v.9)

The Samaritan woman was well aware of the racial tension between her people and the Jews. Read the background of this tension in 2 Kings 17:24–41.

What were the results of this re-settlement of Jews in Samaria, particularly from verses 29 and 33?

John inserts some pertinent information for us in v.9. What is it?

What do you think that means? *(Be sure and notice the actions of the disciples in v.8.)*

Why do you think Jesus chose this Samaritan woman to have this conversation with?

Why do you think the information in v.4 is important?

Verse 18 reveals some aspects of the woman's reputation. What else do we learn from this verse, and how do you think the people of that day viewed this woman?

Verse 27 reveals another cultural aspect of the day. What was that?

What present-day lessons can we glean from Jesus' bridging the culture gap with this woman?

What do you learn from your Savior as He reaches out to those deemed "different" or "less worthy?"

"Receive and experience the amazing grace of the Master, Jesus Christ,
deep, deep within yourselves."
Philippians 4:23 (*The Message*)

Week One - Day 2: The Conversation Takes a Turn

John 4: 9–10

Before you begin…

Prayerfully ask the Lord to speak to you through His Word and to quiet your mind as you learn from Him.

Read the passage for today.

We will spend the bulk of our study time today "dissecting" Jesus' answer to the woman's question in verse 10.

What two components of giving does Jesus reveal in His answer?

_____ of _____

_____ _____

This is Grace: God meeting us at our point of need through the Person of Jesus Christ. Jesus' answer here is power-packed with truth and the <u>revelation of Himself</u>. This is really where our journey of understanding God's grace begins.

Read Romans 5:15–19 to glean a clear understanding.

Paul refers to Adam as a "type" *(v.14 a type is a living prediction or a model of someone who was to come later)* of Christ. He then draws a comparison between the two, the similarities being that their deeds have affected all of humanity.

Compare the two using verses 15–19. (The first one is done for you.)

ADAM	CHRIST
v. 15: Offense	v. 15: Grace
v. 16:	v. 16:
v: 17	v. 17:
v. 18:	v. 18:
v. 19:	v. 19:

In Romans 5:17, we see three truths that can change our lives as we embrace this verse by faith. (Own it; live it.)

How much grace do we receive?

_____

What additional gift do we receive?

_____

What does Jesus empower us to do in life?

_____

This is TRUTH.

Do you believe it?

Are you living it?

Why do we reign in life?

Would you say that you are "reigning in life?"

Take a moment right now to talk with your Heavenly Father about this verse and the reality of it in your life.

In Romans 5:15, 16, and 18, the phrase "the free gift" is mentioned as an aspect of Jesus' salvation of His people. How does this passage align with Jesus' own words in John 4:10 as He converses with the woman?

Who is the focal point of the "gift?"

Based on your study so far, what is the meaning of the phrase, "the gift of God?"

Relate all of this to John 3:16.

GRACE: God meeting me at my point of need through the Person of Jesus Christ and all that His Personhood provides.

"Not only are we saved by grace, we live by it as well."
Streams of Living Water

Richard J. Foster

Week One - Day 3: Living Water

John 4: 10-18

Prayerfully prepare your heart for today's lesson.

Yesterday, we examined part one of Jesus' two-pronged answer to the woman at the well, the "gift of God." Today, we will look at His second part of His answer, "living water."

Before diving into a deeper study, what comes to mind as you read Jesus' words about the "living water?"

Write out your first impressions here:

What does the Bible have to say about "Living Water?" Look up these verses in the Old Testament and briefly summarize each one.

Isaiah 12:3:

Isaiah 44:3 (Note the "I wills"):

Isaiah 55:1:

Zechariah 13:1 (Note "fountain"):

Zechariah 14:8:

Jeremiah 2:13 (What does the Lord call Himself?):

Jeremiah 17:13:

Psalm 36:7–9:

Look up these verses in the New Testament and briefly summarize each one.

John 7:37–39:

Revelation 21:5–7:

Read John 4:10–15. How do all of these verses relate to the <u>message</u> of what Jesus is communicating to the woman?

Do you think the woman initially understood Jesus' teaching on "living water?" Base your answer on her specific responses in verses 11 and 12.

What two things does Jesus promise those who drink from the "water" He offers in v.14?

1. _____

2. _____

Based on your study so far, what do each of the phrases below mean to you?

Questions for Reflection

Put yourself in her sandals…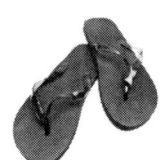

How are you like this woman at this point in our story?

How do you respond to Jesus' statements of the seemingly impossible? (See v.14)

When you receive a fresh word from the Lord (through hearing or your own study), do you then question how it could ever be?

Are you a literalist—so practical that accepting God's word to you, by faith, is something you struggle with?

How's your thirst level? What kinds of things are you thirsting for?

If these questions and your study leave you wanting more of Jesus, more of the "living water," and more depth of relationship with the living Lord, take a moment and confess that to Him right now.

Pour out your heart to your loving Heavenly Father and ask for more "water." He bids us to come and ask (v.10).

How does the woman respond to Jesus' offer of "living water?"

Why do you think she wanted to stop coming to the well?

How does Jesus answer her response?

Do you find this odd? Why or why not?

What do you think is the purpose of Jesus addressing her "husband" issue?

Week One - Day 4: Zoe Life

Diving into the Living Water
John 4

Today we will look at many Scriptures that will broaden our understanding of the "living water" that Jesus spoke of in John 4. Spend some time in prayer asking the Lord to open your heart to His Word. Ask Him to help you set aside your own pre-conceived notions and traditions or any baggage or stereotypes you may carry regarding the "living waters" *(aka the Holy Spirit)*.

Many people get very uptight when the conversation or teaching focuses on the Holy Spirit. Why? What are we afraid of? Jesus wants those of us who belong to Him to be brave and fearless!

As Christ followers, most of us would never deny that we do indeed have the Spirit of the Living God, the resurrection power, resident inside our human frames. After all, it's in the Bible! But have we truly grasped this transforming truth at our soul level to where our lives are characterized by confidence, joy, peace, patience, and power?

Is this our daily experience with the Holy Spirit, or have we mentally assented to His Presence and intellectualized Him?

Have we limited our daily experience of Him to what our church has taught us is culturally acceptable?

Have we remained as a stagnant pool when Jesus has promised us "living water?"

Are we basing what we believe about the Holy Spirit on the comfort of our religious culture and experience, or are we truly living Biblically?

Are you satisfied with the status quo, or does the tantalizing taste of the living water entice you to go deeper with Jesus and all that He offers?

Jesus didn't save us just so we could attend a comfortable church on Sunday, live a moral life, raise well-behaved kids, have a job that is satisfying and sufficient for all our wants and needs (and maybe a tropical vacation or two), and then glide into our sunset years relatively pain-free.

Jesus saved us for the purpose of intimate relationship with Him, by grace, through faith, so that out of this love relationship flows a partnership with Him to build His kingdom.

How can we help build the Kingdom of God without the daily power of God operating in our lives in a transforming way?

The Holy Spirit (*Living Water*) operating in our lives at maximum capacity through our blood-bought relationship with JESUS is what makes us different than any other religion on the earth.

Jesus saved us. He fills us and equips us. Ask Him to make you open and teachable to what the Bible has to say to you today. Are you desperate for more of Him?

There are four Greek words in the New Testament translated "life." The Greek word that Jesus brought to the world is *Zoe*. This means: eternal life and the life of God Himself. Jesus said that words He speaks are spirit and life (Zoe). John 6:63

John's Gospel opens with the word Zoe. Turn to John 1:4 and fill in the blanks:

"In _____ was _____, and the _____ (zoe) was the light of men."

This word is used 130 times in the New Testament.

Read John 10:10 and write out from Jesus' words the <u>what</u> and the <u>type</u> of Zoe Jesus came to bring:

Paul prayed for Christians to be "filled with all the fullness of God" (Eph 3:19). We will learn as we journey together that "all things are possible" due to Zoe, the life of God.

Zoe enables us to be "more than conquerors" and transforms us "from glory to glory."

Zoe is the Source of grace and gives us wisdom, overcoming the "world, the flesh, and the devil."

By filling us with His own Life, God Himself becomes our life, peace, righteousness, purity, strength, health, the preserver of our whole "spirit, soul, and body." (Gal 3:20)

He is our zeal, our joy, our faith, our guide, our teacher—everything that pertains to life and godliness.

How is this possible? Write out your answer based on Romans 5:10.

That's right! All of this abundant Zoe life is made possible through the precious blood of Jesus, shed for us on the cross. Take a moment to thank

Him and worship Him for who He is and what He has done for you.

He didn't just come to save us. He also saved us in order to fill us up with ZOE!! That is grace!! We did nothing to deserve or earn this; it's all a gift.

It is important to understand Zoe because it helps us to better comprehend the "living waters." Another aspect of Zoe and living waters is...

Vine Life
Read John 15:1–11

Jesus calls Himself_____(v.1) and His Father is the
_____(v.1). Jesus calls us _____(v.5).

The Vine's life (Zoe) is in the branches; the life of the branches is directly connected to the Vine. Jesus desires that all of His branches be full of His own life (Zoe).

"He who is joined to the Lord is one spirit with Him."
(1 Cor. 6:17)

Staying connected to the Vine, or <u>abiding,</u> is the key to experiencing more Zoe. Remember, Jesus said in John 4:10, "Just ask and I will give you living water." He wants to fill us with His own life.

In verse 5, what are we able to do without the true vine?

In 2 Corinthians 3:5, where is our sufficiency from?

If this is the case, why do you think we naturally default to relying on ourselves, leaning on our own understanding and doing things our way? (*You can answer this based on your own experience!*)

When we abide in Christ (John 15):

Our prayers are_____v.7.

We glorify_____v.8.

We keep His_____v.10.

We abide in His_____v.10.

We have full_____v.11.

A healthy Vine produces great "fruits" that result from the healthy Vine Zoe-life. See Galatians 5:22–23 and list them here.

1.

2.

3.

4.

5.

6.

7.

8.

9.

God has made His Son the treasury of His fullness. Turn to Colossians 1:19 and fill in the blanks:

"For it pleased the _____ that in _____ (Jesus) all the _____ should _____."

We are united with Christ and joined with Him in spirit, so all of His fullness is now our fullness. Everything that is in the vine flows to the branches! Isn't this amazing?

Then if everything about Jesus and His powerful life is also true of you, do a quick inventory and list everything you know is yours, according to the Bible. Go ahead, rattle it off!

If that doesn't lead you into spontaneous worship and dancing for joy, I don't know what will! Spend some time praising Him right now.

Jesus used very practical illustrations and word pictures to teach the agrarian people of his day the truths of who He is. The Vine and the branches bearing spiritual fruit is a classic example of this. Since it is preserved for us in Scripture, the illustration is meant to teach us today.

Think about a fruit-bearing tree with branches, an apple tree, perhaps. Does that branch stress, strain, labor, or fret to produce its fruit?

_____

Does that healthy branch just produce what comes naturally as it abides in the vine? _____

What would happen to a fruit-bearing branch if an over-zealous pruner came and chopped it off from the vine?

These are elementary questions, but they do cause us to ponder the truth of Jesus' "Vine" teachings in a practical way.

Jesus has promised us the fullness of Himself as we remain in Him. All we need to do is ask and receive. This is our inheritance in Christ. Whenever we sense a lack, we pray to the Giver of Zoe, the Vine life that produces fruit in us, and He gives us more of Himself.

Read Galatians 2:20 and list the truths stated in this powerful verse:

1. _____

2. _____

3. _____

4. _____

5. _____

In Galatians 2:21, Paul says he does not_____ the grace of God.

What does that mean practically, and what are some specific ways to avoid setting aside the grace of God?

In Galatians 3:2, how do we receive the Spirit?

In Galatians 3:3–5 and Galatians 5:16–22, what additional things do you learn about the flesh versus the Spirit?

"I have been crucified with Christ {In Him I have shared His crucifixion}; it is no longer I who live, but Christ {the Messiah} lives in me; and the life I now live in the body I live by faith in {adherence to and reliance on and complete trust in} the Son of God, who loved me and gave Himself up for me. {Therefore, I do not treat God's gracious gift as something of minor importance and defeat its very purpose}; I do not set aside and invalidate and frustrate and nullify the grace {unmerited favor} of God. For if justification {righteousness, acquittal from guilt} comes through {observing the ritual of} the Law, then Christ {the Messiah} died groundlessly and to no purpose and in vain. {His death was then wholly superfluous}." Galatians 2:20 Amplified

While on earth, Jesus said, "Come to me and drink and never thirst again!" From Heaven, He is still urging us with, "I will give of the fountain of the water of life freely to him who thirsts." (Revelation 21:6)

Week One - Day 5: Grace Grows the Church

John 4:19–42

Jesus continues his conversation with the Samaritan woman and they discuss true worship. We then witness the results of what happens when an entire city hears a powerful testimony from a least-likely source.

True Worship. Read verses 19–26.

Who did the woman perceive that Jesus was, and what did she know about worship?

In verses 21–22, what did Jesus teach her about worship?

In verses 23–24, list the things you learn about worship; use the Greek definitions to help you dig deeper.

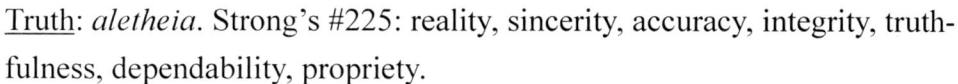

Truth: *aletheia*. Strong's #225: reality, sincerity, accuracy, integrity, truthfulness, dependability, propriety.

Worship: *proskuneo*. Strong's #4352: *pros* means "toward" and *kuneo* means "to kiss," to prostrate oneself, bow down, show reverence, worship, adore.

What amazing thing does Jesus do in verse 26?

The White Harvest Fields. Read verses 27–42.

What does the woman do upon Jesus' revelation?

What are the disciples concerned about?

What new metaphors does Jesus use to teach His disciples about leading others into truth in verses 34–38?

v. 34_____

v. 35_____

v. 36_____

v. 37_____

v. 38_____

What are the results of the woman's testimony?

Relate the events here from verses 39–42.

What is your #1 takeaway from the woman's encounter with Jesus at the well?

You can't argue with testimony.

"There is no one so far lost that Jesus cannot find her and cannot save her."
Andrew Murray

Lesson 2: Grace Heals

Week Two - Day 1: Encounter in a Crowd

Grace Heals
The Woman with the Issue of Blood Encounters Jesus

This week opens up with Jesus Himself encountering the throngs of people and potential followers, but there is one woman who has been battling a lonely illness for twelve years who determines to fight the crowds and seek Jesus out.

"If I can just touch the hem of His garment," she keeps saying to herself, and this is what ultimately propels her to His side. The woman with the issue of blood is a social outcast due to her uncleanness according to Jewish law. For years she spent days on her own, hoping and praying for healing, but she would not receive that healing until she encountered Jesus and His transformational touch.

This week's study examines the Biblical references on healing and the subsequent dynamics that follow. Themes in this study include peace, seeing only with our natural eyes, and traditions and testimony. Not all of the questions we have on healing as believers can be answered, but as you take the time to dive into each verse, a greater understanding of healing will be yours.

Prayerfully prepare your heart as you receive from the Word.

Today's text: Matthew 9:18–22

1. Summarize the events of this passage as they involve this woman.

What are some things that jump out at you from this story?

What surprises you?

What challenges you?

2. How do you see Jesus responding in this narrative?

Turn to Matthew 14:34–36. Who is being brought to Jesus and what are the results?

3. She came from behind and touched the <u>hem of his garment</u>. To better understand the background, deep meaning, and spiritual significance of her action, turn to Numbers 15:37–41.

Who directed the children of Israel to make and wear tassels?

What was the purpose of the tassels?

This visual reminder of the duty to obey the Law was given because of the serious consequences of disobeying the Law.

To see an aspect of the Law that directly impacted the woman, turn to Leviticus 15:19–20 and verse 25.

What was her label according to the Law?

_____

How do you think this impacted her?

      • socially _____

      • emotionally _____

      • spiritually _____

      • physically _____

4. What was the dramatic outcome of this encounter in Matthew's Gospel?

List the ways that this woman's life was transformed by her encounter with Jesus—Grace Personified.

"God wishes to be seen, and He wishes to be sought, and He wishes to be expected, and He wishes to be trusted."

Julian of Norwich

Week Two - Day 2: Grace Sees

Mark 5:21–34

This is the same story of the woman with the blood issue, but Mark gives us a lot more information.

1. What new things do you learn from this passage in regards to the woman? List them here with the verse reference.

2. How do you think she had "heard about Jesus" (v.27) and knew to "touch the hem of his garment?" (v.28)

What drove her to Jesus?

3. What four aspects of her healing do you discover in v.29?

    a)

    b)

    c)

    d)

4. What was Jesus' response to the woman's touch? (verses 30-32)

Cross reference this response with Luke 6:19, and write out what happened as Jesus moved about the people of His day.

What was the disciples' response? (v.31)

Before we are quick to judge the incredulity at Jesus' question, think about our own human tendencies. The disciples most likely answered the same way we would answer, seeing only with our natural eyes when the supernatural Jesus is standing in our midst.

What practical and spiritual lessons can you apply to your own life from the way Jesus responds to this whole situation?

"I know, more surely than I know anything, that any pang of healing or forgiveness or goodness I have ever felt comes solely from the grace of God."

Phillip Yancey

Week Two - Day 3: Grace and Peace

Mark 5:32–34

Prayerfully prepare your heart for today's lesson in the Word.

1. Read the passage for today. Based on what you know of the story and context so far, answer the following questions:
   - In verse 32, what does Jesus do?

   - In verse 33, what is the response of the woman to Jesus' questioning? (See v.31.)

The fact that she knew she had been healed caused her to fall down and worship. Turn to Psalm 89:7 and tell how we see this psalm fulfilled in this very encounter.

• What three things does Jesus declare to her in verse 34?

1.

2.

3.

2. Not only does Jesus heal the woman, but He also gives her peace. His healing of her is both outward and inward. Imagine the lack of peace she has had for twelve years as she has been dealing with this, maintaining her isolation from people because she is unclean.

Turn to Luke 1:78–79 and read the last part of Zacharias's prophecy. In what ways do we see this prophecy fulfilled in this encounter?

Part of Jesus' life purpose was to guide us to peace. Peace: *eirene*. Strong's #1515: A state of rest, quietness, calmness; an absence of strife. *Eirene* includes harmonious relationships between God and men.

Turn to Isaiah 9:6. What is one of the names of Christ?

_____

3. What do you think Jesus means when He tells her in verse 34 that her faith has made her well?

Quite a few verses are listed for you to dig into. Look up these additional Scriptures to help you answer the question above based on what the Word of God says.

Matthew 8:13 _____

Matthew 9:2, 6 _____

Matthew 9:28–29 _____

Matthew 15:26 _____

Mark 1:40–44 _____

Mark 6:5–6 _____

Mark 9:17–24 _____

Mark 10:51–52 _____

Luke 7:44–50 _____

Luke 17:19 _____

Acts 14:8–10 _____

Ephesians 2:8–9 _____

"And He said to her, Daughter, your faith (your trust and confidence in Me, springing from faith in God) has restored you to health. Go in (into) peace and be continually healed *and* freed from your [distressing bodily] disease." Mark 5:34 AMP

"Have you ever thought that in every action of grace in your heart, you have the whole omnipotence of God engaged to bless you?"
Andrew Murray

Week Two - Day 4: Grace Touches

Luke 8:43–48

Prayerfully prepare your heart for today's time in the Word and lesson.

1. Read the passage for today. What <u>new piece</u> of information do you learn from this passage regarding the woman and her situation? (Isn't it interesting that the author of this Gospel, Dr. Luke, would bring this up?)

2. The Greek word for healed is *therapeuo*, where we get our words therapy and therapeutic. The word eventually came to mean to heal, restore to health, to cure. What means had the woman used and ultimately exhausted to find her *therapeuo*? What about you? Do you have a story to tell in regards to your own healing? What is your natural and normal response/reaction when you have a health issue?

3. In verse 44, we learn that the woman came from <u>behind</u> to touch Jesus. Why do you think she did that, based on your study so far?

4. In verse 45, Jesus asks, "Who touched me?" Do you think the Sovereign Lord knew who touched Him, or do you think he needed to ask? Why or why not?

5. List the events that followed after Jesus' question. After you've finished your list, tell why you think Jesus had to ask the question, "Who touched me?"

"The purpose of grace is primarily to restore our relationship with God. The work of grace aims at an ever deeper knowledge of God and an ever closer fellowship with him. Grace is God drawing us to himself."

J.I. Packer

<u>Declare</u>: *apaggello* Strong's #518: To announce, to bring word, report, show, tell.

| Questions for Reflection | Put yourself in her sandals…  |

What is your life—testimony—witness—declaring about Jesus today?

Do your <u>words</u> reveal His grace?

Do you <u>report</u> on His grace, mercy, and healing in your life?

Does your lifestyle <u>show</u> His grace and your subsequent faith?

Do you consistently <u>tell</u> others about your wonderful Jesus?

"I give thanks to God with everything I've got. God's works are so great, worth a lifetime of study—endless enjoyment! His generosity never gives out. He's so personal and holy, worthy of our respect."

Psalm 111:1–3, 10 (*The Message*)

Week Two - Day 5: Biblical Healing

What the Bible Has to Say about Healing

For many of us, our beliefs about divine healing may have been formed by a variety of sources: personal experience with (or without) healing, teaching we've received, personal Bible study, cultural traditions, denominational traditions and beliefs, or even things we've witnessed on TV or throughout our lives or stories we've heard and read.

When we journey through the Gospels and encounter Jesus for ourselves—Grace Personified, we are confronted with His healing ministry. These are amazing stories, but does He still heal today? Did He heal in the Gospels as an aspect of revealing himself as Savior of the world? Even though His apostles still performed miracles after He ascended to heaven, was that just for the "apostolic age" so the early church could be birthed? Is it not for today, since now we're in the "church age" and we have the Bible in its entirety, so we don't need miracles, including healing?

No matter how you answer these questions, it's essential that your beliefs are based on what the Bible has to say, not what you've experienced or have not experienced. Paul commended the Bereans in Acts 17:10–12. What two things did the Bereans do when they were taught?

1.

2.

Let's take a moment right now and ask the Holy Spirit to reveal Jesus to you through God's Word. Ask Him to make you open and teachable to what His Word reveals. Ask Him to make you a "Berean."

We all know many people who have prayed for healing and then did not live. These people were precious to us: grandparents, spouses, friends, and even children. The devastating loss of these loved ones can leave us with deep questions—why—or why not? Sometimes we see immediate glory and fruit as a result of their passing and this can be a comfort to us in our grief, but ultimately, we are still left with a gaping hole in our lives of where that precious one used to be, and their absence is felt keenly for years.

Who can know the mind of the Lord? His ways and thoughts are so much higher than ours, we are told in the Scriptures.

Even in the Scriptures, we can see a long list of testimonies of great people of faith in Hebrews 11, and at the end of that passage we read that many died_____v.39.

Read Hebrews 11:36–40.

We cannot always answer the "why" questions of life and death this side of heaven, but we can know the "what." God is always good, completely sovereign, merciful, just, pure, holy, and loving.

Tradition

J. I. Packer writes, "Nobody can claim to be detached from traditions. In fact, one sure way to be swallowed up by traditionalism is to think that one is immune to it…the question then, is not whether we *have* traditions, but whether our traditions conflict with the only absolute standard in these matters: Holy Scripture. All Christians are at once beneficiaries and victims of tradition—beneficiaries, who receive nurturing truth and wisdom from God's faithfulness in past generations; victims, who now take for granted things that need to be questioned, thus treating as divine absolutes patterns of belief and behavior that should be seen as human, provisional, and relative. We are all beneficiaries of good, wise, and sound tradition, and victims of poor, unwise, and unsound tradition."

"The Comfort of Conservatism" in *Power Religion,* ed. Michael Horton (Chicago: Moody Press, 1992) p. 286–290.

1. As you explore these Scriptures, keep in mind some key things about the Word itself.

1 Peter 1:23. The Word is an_____.

Proverbs 4:20–23. List the things we are to do with the Word:

James 1:22, We are to be_____ of the Word.

2. Utilize this time as a worship time, praising God for who He is.

- What is the Old Testament name of God given to us in Exodus 15:26?

- Why did Jesus say He came in Luke 4:18–19?

- Do you think illness, sickness, affliction, pain, and disease would be included under the "oppression" category? Why or why not?

3. What do you learn about God in Malachi 3:6?

4. What do you learn about Jesus in Hebrews 13:8?

How do these two Biblical revelations impact the fact that one of the very names of God is "Healer?"

How does this impact your beliefs on Biblical healing?

If neither God the Father nor God the Son ever change, would <u>that</u> in and of itself be reason enough biblically to believe He still heals today?

1.   Have you allowed your personal experiences to cast doubt upon the teaching of God's Word? Do you believe that Jesus' atoning death on the cross provided for not only our salvation but also our healing? Why or why not?

Look up the following Scriptures and summarize the truth of each one:

Isaiah 53:4–5:

Matthew 8:16–17:

(How many did He heal who were sick?)

Psalm 103:1–5:

Galatians 3:13:

What did Christ become for us?

Deuteronomy 28:15–62. List the specific curses:

(If you don't have time to read all these verses, please note especially 21, 22, 27, 35, and 61.)

What kinds of sicknesses are included because of the curse of the Law, according to these verses?

• What did Jesus become for us on the cross?

2.   To conclude your study time today, look up these verses and write out any truth or principle that the Lord illuminates for you in a fresh way in the space provided.

Genesis 20:17:

Luke 9:1–2:

Exodus 23:25:

Luke 13:10–13:

Psalm 107:20:

John 5:5–8:

Proverbs 3:5–8:

John 9:1–7:

Isaiah 57:15, 18:

Acts 28:8–9

Matthew 4:23:

Romans 8:11:

Matthew 8:14–15:

1 Thessalonians 5:23:

Matthew 12:15:

James 5:14–16:

Acts 10:38:

3 John 1:2:

What are your Biblical conclusions about healing for today?

"Rock of Ages cleft for me, let me hide myself in thee. Let the water and the blood, from thy wounded side, which flowed. Be of sin the <u>double</u> cure, save from wrath and make me pure." Augustus Toplady, 1775

Lesson 3: Grace Catches

Testimonies, Throngs, and Transformational Touch

Week Three - Day 1: Encounter in the Temple

The Adulterous Woman Encounters Jesus
John 8: 2–2

Who would have thought that a story about an adulterous woman would actually take place in the Jewish temple of Jesus' day? This encounter exposes the hearts of the Jewish law-keepers, the Pharisees, and their desire to trick or trap Jesus in His own theology. Their plan backfires as Jesus responds to the woman caught in adultery in an unconventional manner.

The setting of the temple provides one of our greatest lessons as we see in a fresh way that Jesus came to write His law on our hearts. Adultery and infidelity are common and widespread sins in our culture today. This encounter reminds us that there is nothing new under the sun, and the true Son has the answers for all of us. The answer is not the law, but rather, more grace.

Take the time this week to discover the contrasts between the law and the promises of God (grace). Experience in a fresh way how grace really does free us!

Prayerfully prepare your heart for today's lesson.

1) Describe the scene in verse 2. This piece of the story is important!

2) Tell about the characters in our story who enter the scene in verse 3. Write down everything you already know about the Scribes and Pharisees.

Pharisees in "pho-cus"

3) Look up the following Scriptures and write out things you learn about Pharisees and teachers of the Law:

Mark 7:3:

Matthew 15:3–4:

Matthew 23:3:

Matthew 23:29–30; 31–32

Luke 18:11–12:

Matthew 23:33:

Matthew 21:23:

Matthew 9:11:

Luke 16:15:

4) Read verses 4–6 again. What is the motive of the Pharisees?

5) Do you think they respect Jesus? Why or why not?

6) Look up Leviticus 20:10 and tell about the Law and the consequences for violating it.

7) How did Jesus respond to their entrance onto the scene and their questioning of Him?

Do you find His response odd? Why do you think Jesus did this?

"God delights to meet the faith of one who looks up to Him and says,
'Lord, You know that I cannot do this—but I believe that you can!'"
Amy Carmichael

Week Three - Day 2: Grace Stoops

John 8:7–12

1. In verses 7 and 8, list out all of the actions done by Jesus, knowing that nothing in God's Word is ever wasted. All of His Word is preserved for us on purpose. What do you think is the significance of Jesus' posture in these verses?

2. Verse 9 is the critical turning point in our story. Tell in your own words what happens to the very ones who brought the accused woman to Jesus.

3. Turn to and read Paul's difficult words to the strict keepers of the Law in Romans 2:17–24. List the dominant things you see in these verses that the Pharisees in our passage were also guilty of. (The first one is done for you.)

v.17: Rested on the Law

v.18:

v.19:

v.20:

v.21:

v.22:

v.23:

v.24:

1. What is the difference between being "convicted by their conscience" and being convicted by the word of the Lord?

2. What are the two questions Jesus asks of the woman in verse 10?

3. What two actions did the Pharisees take toward the woman?

Read:

Matthew 7:1–2: How does God feel about judging?

John 8:44: Who is our enemy, and what does he do to us?

1. What two things did Jesus say to the woman?

2. What do you think Jesus thinks of her sin?

3. How did Jesus reveal Himself in the passage in verse 12? How was this woman "walking in darkness" prior to coming to Jesus and encountering His grace?

Questions for Reflection	Put yourself in her sandals…

How do you think the woman felt when she was brought to the temple by the Pharisees?

Have you ever been in a public situation where you were humiliated in front of a group?

If so, how did you deal with that?

Have you ever been accused?

How do you think the woman felt when Jesus engaged her in conversation?

How does this Biblical story impact you personally?

"When we focus on God, the scene changes. He's in control of our lives; nothing lies outside the realm of His redemptive grace. Even when we make mistakes, fail in relationships, or deliberately make bad choices, God can redeem us."
Penelope Stokes

Week Three - Day 3: Grace Rocks!

Before the woman "caught in the act of adultery" encountered Jesus, she encountered the Pharisees and the teachers of the law. These religious leaders were the personification of the law, while Jesus is Grace Personified.

Grace: *Charis,* **Strong's #5485:** Divine favor and blessing; that brings joy, pleasure, delight, loveliness, grace of speech, good will, loving-kindness. The divine influence upon the heart and its reflection in life.

Gift: *Charisma:* A divine gratuity; deliverance from danger or passion; spiritual endowment; miraculous faculty.

Before we can fully appreciate grace and all it means for us, we need to take a long, hard look at the Law and how it figures into our particular story as well as the story of our own lives. As you study today, ask the Lord to teach you through His Word and to make you even more aware of His wonderful gift of salvation to you by grace, through faith.

1) What is the purpose of the Law according to Romans 7:7?

2) What does Scripture say is the condition of those under the Law in Galatians 3:10?

3) In Galatians 3:19, we are taught that the law was _____ because of _____ (sin).

4) Turn to Exodus 20:1–17. Read the law for yourself. In this list, who is
the one that is doing all of the action?

5) It's been said that at first sin is pleasing, then it becomes easy, then delightful, then frequent, and then it is a full-blown habit. Read Romans
6:23. What is the <u>wage</u> of sin? _____

- A <u>wage</u> was a ration or stipend originally given to a soldier in
military service. Today, a wage is something that is owed to us;
payment for work done; recompense.

- Read Romans 6:16, 20. The Greek word for slave in these verses is
doulos, which comes from "to bind"—denoting bondage or subjec-
tion to slavery. Very often the service involved is voluntary—will-
ingly becoming in bondage to whatever entices you.
- Read John 8:34. Summarize from your brief study of these verses
and word meanings what sin does to us.

6) Back to our story…another hard look at what the Bible has to say about the sin of adultery.

- Read Galatians 5:16–17, 19. What is at war with our walk in the Spirit? List the works of the flesh:

- Are the works of the flesh, for the Christian, what we really <u>want</u> to do?

- Read Romans 7:19–24 to discover your answer and Paul's testimony, too.

In our passage with the woman (John 8:3), the Greek word in this verse for adultery is *moicheia* (Strong's #3430). The word means unlawful sexual intercourse, illicit connection with a married person; marital infidelity.

When Paul lists the works of the flesh in Galatians (see question above), he begins with adultery. Adultery also comes from the Greek word *porneia,* which includes <u>all sexual activity</u> outside of marriage.

Throughout the New Testament, when referring to a woman who has committed adultery, the word generally used is *pornos*. This word describes any woman who has committed adultery and, it is the same word for prostitute. When referring to a man who has committed adultery, *porneia* means he had sexual relations with a prostitute. This term does not <u>only</u> refer to a professional prostitute where money was exchanged, but that the two involved "prostituted themselves" (sold) to the sin of illicit sexual relations.

The word <u>pornography</u> comes from the same Greek word which means <u>mental prostitution.</u> This sheds new light on what Jesus said in Matthew 5:28. Write out the verse here:

7) From your study, summarize what you've learned about sin, the Law, and God's view of it all.

Week Three - Day 4: Grace Fulfills

Sin <u>works</u> you, but Grace <u>saves</u> you!

Yesterday's study of the Law probably left all of us feeling heavy and hopeless. Today we will see Jesus' relationship to the Law and His active grace in our lives. Our personal grace encounter changes everything!

1) What did Jesus say about His response to the law in Matthew 5:17? Write out the verse here:

The Greek word for fulfill—*plerosai*—means to bring about the event to which the Law and the prophets pointed.

2) We learned yesterday that the law was "added" (see again Romans 5:20 and Galatians 3:19) after the _____ (look up Galatians 3:8) was preached to_____ .

3) The promise made to Abraham was actually the _____! What did Jesus say about this in John 8:56?

4) Turn again to Galatians 3:19 to answer the following questions:

- What purpose does the Law serve?

- Who was the seed?

- What was the promise?

"Jesus showed by His statement of fulfilling the Law, that it was incomplete without Him arriving on the scene! The law was always unfinished business until Jesus came. Abraham knew that what had been promised to him would be <u>fulfilled</u> by a Person traceable to himself."

Grace

R.T. Kendall

5) Read Galatians 3:20–24. List all the facts you glean from these five verses, contrasting the Law and the promises of God (grace).

6) Read Romans 6:4–18, an amazing passage explaining to us how Christ did for us what the law could not do. List the truths of our inheritance from this passage as bullet points: (The first one is done for you.)
- I was buried with Christ through His baptism. v.4
- I walk in newness of life. v.4

This is your inheritance! Read your list out loud to God in praise and worship to Him for what He gave you through JESUS!

"Don't we all long for a father who cares for us in spite of our failures? We do have that type of a father. A father who is at His best when we are at our worst—whose grace is strongest when our devotion is weakest."
Max Lucado

Week Three - Day 5: Grace Frees

I hope that by this point of your study you are brimming over with joy and gratitude for your own grace encounter with the living Lord! We have seen that there is nothing wrong with the Law, but there's a lot wrong with us—without a Savior!

Today's focus is all on JESUS! Because He lives, we live, and we walk in newness of life.

1) Read Romans 8:1–5 and answer the following questions:

• Should we ever feel condemnation as a Christian?

• How are we to walk?

• What has the Law of the Spirit done for you?

• What did God do for you?

• How is the righteous requirement of the Law met in you?

• How do you practically set your mind on things of the spirit?

2) Another look at condemnation. Read John 3:17-18 and John 9:56. Why did Jesus come?

Spend some time thanking and praising Him.

3) Read and list in bullet points everything you learn about the New Covenant that Jesus brought with Him in Hebrews 8:7–12.

For Review

To solidify your understanding of Law and Grace, review your last two days of study and fill in the contrast chart below from everything you've gleaned.

Law—Pharisess	Grace—Jesus
• accuse	• accept
• condemn	• no condemnation
• thou shalt not	• "I will..."

Amazing Grace, how sweet the sound! My chains are gone; I've been set free.

Lesson 4: Grace Yields Faith and Worship

The Woman Caught in Adultery

Week Four - Day 1: Grace Yields Faith and Worship

Mary of Bethany Encounters Jesus

This week of study is shared by two women in the Bible named Mary: Mary of Bethany and Mary the mother of Jesus. Mary of Bethany provides us with the beautiful example of devotion and teachability. She is deliberate in her action of sitting at the feet of Jesus, but this does not come without a cost to her. Through this encounter, we learn about the futility of worry and why Jesus is anti-worry. We also learn about the significance of Bethany. You won't want to miss a single aspect of this encounter with one of Jesus' best friends while He was on the earth.

Jesus' mother, Mary, also provides us with a profound example of receiving the Word of God and believing it, thus living a life of supernatural proportions. The encounter starts out with a conversation between Mary and an angel. We examine this conversation at length and glean some life-changing applications from it. We take a Biblical look at what it means for the Holy Spirit to overshadow a person and how that has relevance for us today.

Mary of Bethany had several encounters with Jesus because she, her sister Martha, and her brother Lazarus were very good friends with Jesus. We will study one of these encounters in-depth for the purpose of our study. If you would like to read of her other encounters with Jesus, the references are listed for you here:

- John 11:1–45: Jesus raises Lazarus from the dead.
- Matthew 26:6–13 and John 12:1-8: Mary anoints Jesus.

1) Read the passage for today in Luke 10:38–42. List all of your observations about Martha from this passage.

- List all of your observations about Mary from this passage.

- What differences do you see between the two sisters? What similarities?

2) In verse 39, what two specific ways does Mary demonstrate her devotion to Jesus?

3) In verse 40, what two specific ways does Martha demonstrate her distraction from Jesus?

Questions for Reflection

Put yourself in her sandals…

1. Where do you see yourself in light of these two women in our story? Do you identify more with Mary or with Martha, or somewhere in between?

2. Are you, like Mary, sitting at His feet? Are you hearing from Him? What does it mean to really hear from Jesus? What does it take for you to sit and hear?

3. Do the following acrostic, filling in each letter reflecting practical aspects of being a worshiper like Mary.

S —   H —

I —   E —

T —   A —

                        R —

"Faith is a living, daring confidence in God's grace, so sure and certain that a man could stake his life on it a thousand times."
Martin Luther

Week Four - Day 2: Grace Frees

Luke 10:38-42

1) Read the passage for today again. What was Jesus' response to Martha in verse 41?

Worry: *Merimnao* (Strong's #3309): "To divide into parts." The word suggests a distraction, a preoccupation with things causing anxiety, stress. and pressure.

In what specific ways was Martha "divided" into parts while Mary had <u>one</u> purpose?

Jesus' intent was to free Martha and all of us from our worries, concerns, to-do lists, and all of the "what-ifs" in life. He specifically instructed all of us <u>not to</u> <u>worry,</u> and Paul echoed this command in Philippians 4: "Do not be anxious about anything!"

Turn to Matthew 6:25–34, and read Jesus' classic words on worry. I've given you the "5-UN's" of worry with the verse reference. Next to it, list why we are not to worry.

a) Worry is <u>unreasonable</u> (v.25).

b) Worry is <u>unnatural</u> (v.26).

c) Worry is <u>unhelpful</u> (v.27).

d) Worry is <u>unnecessary</u> (v.30).

e) Worry is <u>unbelief</u> (v.31–32).

2) What did Jesus say Mary had done in verse 42?

3) What do you think is the "good" part she chose?

4) Why do you think Mary made that choice and Martha did not?

Turn to Psalm 27:4 and write the verse here.

How does this verse resonate with what Jesus is calling "good" here?

Turn to John 6:27 and write the verse here.

How does this verse align with Mary and her choice?

5) Jesus declared that Mary had chosen something that could "not be taken away from her." What do you think He meant by that? Write your thoughts here.

6) For another possibility, turn to Mark 4:1–20. Read the parable of the Sower. What are the four types of <u>soil</u> and their descriptions the Sower sowed on?

a)

b)

c)

d)

• What happened to each <u>type of soil</u>, and <u>why</u> did it happen to that soil?

a)

b)

c)

d)

• What type of soil do you think Mary had and why?

• At the risk of being a tad bit critical, what type of soil do you think
Martha had and why? (Remember, Jesus had already told her she was

worried and troubled.)

• Why do you think Jesus was anti-worry?

• What does worry reveal about us?

Our faith?

Our relationship with Jesus?

• What type of soil are you?

• What "camp" are you in now after your two-day study of Mary and Martha?

• How did Mary's encounter with grace transform her life?

• How has <u>your</u> encounter with Grace transformed <u>your</u> life?

"Grace and gratitude belong together like heaven and earth. Grace evokes gratitude like the voice of an echo. Gratitude follows grace as thunder follows lightning."
Karl Barth

Week Four - Day 3: Grace Fulfilled

Mary Encounters Jesus as His Mother
Luke 1:26–45

Read the text for today's lesson.

1. List all of the facts about the "messenger" in verse 26, and read Psalm 103:20 for additional information.

2. List the four things the angel declared to Mary in verse 28:

a)

b)

c)

d)

What was Mary's initial response in verse 29?

The King James Version says: "She was troubled at his saying, and <u>cast it in her mind</u> what manner of salutation this should be."

The Greek transliteration for <u>cast in her mind</u> is *dialogizomai* (you can see our word "dialog" in that word), which means: to reckon thoroughly; to deliberate by reflection or discussion; to consider, dispute, muse, reason, to think.

Questions for Reflection	Put yourself in her sandals… 

How do you think you would respond if an angel came into your home and personally greeted you with a message from God?

Do you think you would "cast in your mind" or have a mental dialog with yourself, too?

Is it our human tendency to be troubled in our minds when things are beyond our ability to understand them?

How does this aspect of the narrative reveal Mary's humanity? (Elisha was a man just like us!)

In verses 30–33, the angel tells Mary ten things. List them here with the verse reference. The first one is done for you.

1) Do not be afraid, v.30 (usually the first thing an angel says).

2) _____

3) _____

4) _____

5) _____

6) _____

7) _____

8) _____

9) _____

10) _____

The position of Jesus as the heir to the throne of David and of His eternal kingdom identify Him as the promised Messiah. List the prophecy from Isaiah 9:6–7.

- How does this correlate to the angel's prophecy?

- Write down the significant things you learn from Hebrews 1:1–9 about Jesus.

Week Four - Day 4: Grace Overshadows

Luke 1:34–45

1) Read the text for today. Even though Mary had the unique experience of a visit from an angel heralding a message directly from God for her (Day 3, Question 3), why do you think she had trouble grasping it? To answer, use verses 27 and 34.

- What does this tell us about how we humans view our circumstances?

2) What did the angel tell Mary would happen to her in verse 35?

Cross reference Matthew 1:18–23 and see what was happening to Mary's betrothed at the same time.

3) The conception of our Lord and Savior Jesus Christ took place by the direct work of the Holy Spirit's power. The word "overshadow" used in this verse is the same word used to describe the Lord's presence in Exodus 40:34–38. Turn there now and read that reference, and then answer the following questions:

The Glory of the Lord filled the Tabernacle…

What covered the tabernacle?

v.34_____

Why was Moses not able to enter the tabernacle?

v.35_____

What would the Israelites do when the cloud was taken up?

_____

What was over the tabernacle by night?

_____

John 1:14 says, "The Word became flesh and <u>dwelt</u> (or *tabernacled*) among us, and we beheld His glory, the glory as of the only begotten of the Father, full of grace and truth."

Isn't it amazing how we have learned that JESUS is the fulfillment of all things? He fulfilled the Law, and in fact, fulfills the entire Old Testament!

God gave His people a tangible picture thousands of years before Christ: the tabernacle was symbolic of the Lord's presence, His dwelling among the people. The Glory of the Lord (the cloud) is symbolic of the Holy Spirit and His power overshadowing the tabernacle. JESUS the begotten came and *tabernacled* among us!

His very *conception* was implemented by the overshadowing (the cloud) of the powerful Holy Spirit. His birth and thirty-three years of life yielded a new tent or tabernacle among us.

Take a few minutes to worship Him right now for being the fulfillment of everything and your own personal fulfillment. Grace Fulfills!

4) Mary's questioning of the angel Gabriel was not one of unbelief like Zacharias in Luke 1:18: "How shall I know this?" (see also Luke 1:19–20) Mary's question was wanting to understand how she, a virgin, could give birth to the Messiah. How did the angel answer her in verse 37?

•   Write out Jeremiah 32:17 for an Old Testament twist on the same message.

"How could I be anything but quite happy if I believed always that all the past is forgiven, all the present is furnished with power, and all the future bright with hope."

James Smetham

Week Four - Day 5: Grace Poured Out

Luke 1:38–45

Yesterday we continued our study of Mary's conversation with the angel, Gabriel. He encouraged her faith in verses 36–37 by informing her of Elizabeth, her barren cousin, also with child, and how nothing—nothing—is impossible with God!

1. What was Mary's response to the angel in verse 38?

The "word" in this verse is transliterated *rhema*: that which is said or spoken; an utterance. In contrast to *logos*, which is the expression of a thought or message, *rhema* is the communication of that message.

In regards to the Bible, *Logos* is the Bible in its entirety; *rhema* is a distinct verse out of the *logos* that is quickened to us by the Holy Spirit.

Mary responded to the *rhema*—the distinct message or word from God with a heart of faith: "May it be to me as you have said" (spoken, uttered). She chose to believe God's word (*rhema*) over her physical circumstances (not knowing a man).

2. Continue reading the entire text for today. What was Elizabeth's response to Mary's faith, and what did she prophetically declare in verse 45?

The word fulfillment or performance in this verse means completion of prophecy, verification, perfection. As for God his way is _____ Psalms 18:30. Every good and _____ gift is from above. James 1:17. _____ love casts out fear. 1 John 4:18. The Lord, He will _____ that which concerns me. Psalms 138:8

1) What does God say about His Word in Isaiah 55:11?

When God's Word of promise is received, it will never be barren. The power in His Word will always fulfill the promise of His Word.

Romans 10:17 declares that "_____comes by hearing, and hearing by the _____ of _____."

What word (*rhema*) have you received throughout your study this week or any of the previous weeks? How has this blessed you or challenged you?

2) What two things happened to Elizabeth as soon as she heard Mary's greeting in v.41?

- How was this event the fulfillment of what the angel had spoken to Zacharias in Luke 1:13–17?

- Who was the angel who spoke with Zacharias? (v.19)

- Who was the angel that spoke to Mary? (v.26)

- Who was the angel that foretold of Messiah's coming in Daniel 9:25?

- What will happen when Christ returns according to 1 Thessalonians 4:16? (Do you think Gabriel will get the honors?)

The angel heralded John's coming to Zacharias. John's name means "the Lord has shown favor (grace)." This was the significance of John's life and purpose: He (John), the one who had been shown grace, would live to prepare the way, for the gift of God's grace, JESUS. John's ministry would be characterized by the fullness of the Holy Spirit (John 1:15), even from his mother's womb (John 1:41). This had not been seen in Scripture before. Prior to this time, the Holy Spirit's outpouring (or filling) was usually reserved for spiritual and national leaders of Israel. This Holy Spirit filling of John was symbolic of the New Covenant age when all believers would be filled. (These teaching points inspired by the Spirit-Filled Life NKJV Bible.)

3) What did Jesus say about the Holy Spirit before His crucifixion in John 16:7 and 13–15? List them here.

4) What were Jesus' final instructions to His disciples in Acts 1:4–8?

• What actually occurred in Acts 2:1–4?

• What was spoken by the prophet Joel according to Peter's sermon in Acts 2:16–21?

This entire week has been dominated by a focus on the preeminence of the Word of God in our lives. Jesus, the Living Word, was the center of Mary of Bethany's life. She deliberately took the time to sit at the feet of Jesus, the Word. Mary, His mother, believed the word spoken to her and she was blessed.

As she took the Living Word inside of her to visit her cousin, accompanied by her faith, the Holy Spirit was uniquely poured out in Elizabeth's life, ushering in a new age of prophecy via her son, John. This new age would yield the greatest gift of all, the gift of grace—JESUS. It is clear from Scripture in both Old and New Testaments that God has always wanted to tabernacle with His people—He has always wanted relationship.

JESUS, Grace, provides that encounter for all of us.

What has been your biggest take away from your brief four-week study of *Grace Encounters*?

What new things have you learned about:

- The Holy Spirit (Living Water)?

- Biblical views on healing?

- The Law vs. Grace?

- The place of the Word in our lives?

- Worship?

"The Lord's chief desire is to reveal himself to you and, in order for Him to do that, He gives you abundant grace... He touches you, and His touch is so delightful that, more than ever, you are inwardly drawn to Him."

Madame Guyon

Epilogue: The End of Our Journey

You have come to the end of your four-week journey of peering into the lives of five women who met Jesus face-to-face. I hope that you have gleaned treasures from this study that you'd never seen before. And I hope, too, that your own personal encounter with Jesus has been enriched and deepened.

I hope that you've seen in a fresh way, that as we journey through this life, and as we relate to Jesus each day, we are to trust His goodness and not our good behavior. We can do this because His experience has become our spiritual history. His historic death on the cross settled forever any debt we owed due to our behavior. As we embrace Him as Lord and Savior, He endows to us all that we could ever need. He makes us acceptable to God, and we take on His righteousness.

This is truly the definition of Grace: God meeting me at my point of need through the Person of Jesus Christ and all that He provides. "Therefore, having been justified by faith, we have peace with God through our Lord Jesus Christ, through whom also we have access by faith into this grace in which we stand, and rejoice in the hope of the glory of God." (Romans 5:1-2)

All of Scripture is meant to lead us to an encounter with Jesus. In every story, God reveals His nature, and embedded in that story, is an invitation to know Him experientially the same way. Mary, the mother of Jesus, believed the Word of God over her impossible circumstances. We can determine to believe the Word of the Lord like Mary, and as we do, there will be a fulfillment of those things which have been spoken to us from the Word. These five women who encountered Jesus had no spiritual advantage over us. You and I have the same grace and intimacy with Him available to us today.

Bibliography

Bosworth, F.F. *Christ the Healer*. Grand Rapids: Revell Publishing, 2005.

Deere, Jack. *Surprised By the Power of the Spirit*. Grand Rapids: Zondervan Publishing, 1993.

Kendall, R.T. *Grace*. Lake Mary: Charisma House Publishing, 2006.

Prince, Joseph. *Destined To Reign*. Tulsa: Harrison House Publishing, 2008.

Renner, Rick. *Sparkling Gems from the Greek*. Tulsa: Teach All Nations Publishing, 2003.

Strong, James, (Corrected by John R. Kohlenberger, III and James A. Swanson). The Strongest Strong's Exhaustive Concordance of the Bible. Grand Rapids: Zondervan, 2001.

About the Author

Marjie Schaefer was born in Georgia, raised in Texas, and has spent the past three decades in the state of Washington. She and her husband, Steve, who this past year celebrated their twenty-fourth year of marriage, have four children: daughter Hayley, and sons Jordan, Matthew, and Luke. Marjie has had the privilege of being a stay-at-home mom for the past twenty-one years and considers this a great blessing.

Marjie describes herself as an everyday girl who loves Jesus and daily pursues a life with Him at the center of her activities and purposes. She started leading and teaching Bible studies while a student at Washington State University and has continued to open her home and her life to anyone who wants more of the Word and more of Jesus. Her greatest passion is bringing the Word of God to life through practical application and visual tools. Women look forward to her personal touches while attending her studies, and they usually go home with laminated verses and other tangible reminders of God's love for them.

At the encouragement of her godly mother, Marjie began spending deliberate and daily time in the Word of God while she was a young girl. This has given her a foundation that has stood the test of time. She began writing her own Bible studies at the request of friends who desired to study the Word during the summer months. *Grace Encounters* is a result of that request.

Do You Want To Encounter More?

If you enjoyed this Bible study and would like to have the opportunity to hear more from Marjie and her teaching, be sure and visit her website:

http://GraceEncounters.com

Read more about the study you just completed and make sure you sign up at my site to be notified of all updates to this Bible study.

On the http://GraceEncounters.com website, you can purchase additional copies of *Grace Encounters* for yourself or others. Marjie would love to hear how the study impacted your life, so be sure to post a comment.

Connect with Marjie through Her Blog

Marjie also has a weekly blog post where she shares current happenings and reflections from her life. Be sure and sign up to have her weekly newsletter sent directly to your email box.

http://www.MarjieSchaefer.com/blog

Connect with Marjie through Twitter

To follow Marjie and her daily tweets sent through Twitter, you can get notified via your phone, electronic device, or computer. Her desire is to share more on the subject of grace via 140 characters. Her Twitter name is: @followmarjie

CPSIA information can be obtained at www.ICGtesting.com
Printed in the USA
BVOW030103101011

273165BV00001B/63/P